Written by Lauren K Carlson

Images attributed:

pg 4 rawpixel.com   pg 6 aslerromero-freepix.com   pg 7-8 freepik.com   pg 9 pressfoto-freepik.com
pg 13 freepik.com   pg 15 pressfoto-freepik.com   pg 17 rawpixel.com   pg 18-19 freepik.com
pg 20 katemangostar- freepik.com   pg 21 creativeart-freepik.com   pg 25 freepik.com, rawpixel.com,
yanalya-freepik.com   pg 26-27 freepik.com, Iconicbestiary-freepik.com   pg 28 pressfoto-freepik.com
pg 29 aslerromero-freepik.com   pg 33 pressfoto-freepik.com, jcomp-freepik.com
pg 34 racool_studio-freepik.com   pg 35 rawpixel.com   pg 36 freepik.com

Cover designed using images of starline-freepik.com/freepik.com/rawpixel.com

But Did I Say YES
Grade 6-8

Introduction	1
Section 1- My Body, My Boundaries	11
Section 2- Respecting Boundaries	23
Section 3- Sexual Assault	31
Review	39

Introduction

Note to Students,

The purpose of this workbook is to guide a conversation about topics that are vital to the safety and healthy growth of our youth. This is not a sexuality education class.

In this class we will talk about the social and emotional aspects of sexuality. I can guarantee that at some point during the completion of this workbook, someone in this room will be embarrassed. Someone in this room will giggle. What we won't do is embarrass other students. This workbook is about teaching RESPECT! And the respect starts right here, right now in this room. Anything less has no place here.

Take a minute to close your eyes and take a few deep breaths. When you open your eyes, you will be in a safe place. Within this workbook, you may decide to share stories or feelings that are important to you. Some of you may not. But know that you have a safe place here.

We will respect each other. We will respect ourselves and we will respect the lessons that are laid out in this workbook.

Thank you.

HUSTLE UP

Today is your first basketball practice. New team, new coach and you can't wait to start learning plays and perfecting your skills on the court. Your coach blows his whistle and shouts to your team to start warming up. He says, "Line up! Let's start with some knee-up jumpy-shots!"

No one moves. Probably because no one knows what a "knee-up jumpy-shot" is. Everyone just stares.

Coach blows his whistle again. "HUSTLE UP! How about some far-out-long-shots?" Your teammates are silent.   Your coach yells,

"Skippy-Scoots?"

"Skoodle Throws?"

"Paddle Wags?"

COME ON GUYS!! DON'T YOU KNOW BASKETBALL?!"

What happened in this scenario?

What issues in communication can you see here?

Proper Vocabulary

Accurate vocabulary leads to effective communication, no matter the topic. Properly naming anatomy eliminates misunderstandings when discussing concerns or questions about your body or puberty. Read the words below and understand that while they may not be appropriate in all contexts, all of us should be able to say these words.

NOT BAD WORDS

- Period
- Penis
- Menstruation
- Testicle
- Anus
- Vagina
- Sex
- Nipple
- Labia
- Rape
- Breast

Trusted Adults

Trusted adults are people you are comfortable with when you have an important question. It is important to have someone you can go to when you have a concern. This person is probably a good listener and cares about you. Imagine yourself revealing something difficult or embarrassing. Who can you trust?

_____
_____

All adults are trusted in different ways. You may trust some adults with questions about relationships or friendships while trusting others with questions about your body. Who can you go to if you have questions about puberty or concerns about your body?

_____
_____

Critical Thinking...

Why is it important to have more than one trusted adult in your life?

My Body

You are your own person and you are in control of your own body. This means that you are aware you have rights and your body is your own. Let's start by exploring what this DOESN't mean.

This **DOESN'T** mean...

- you can break the law with illegal substances

- you can decide that you are old enough to drive

- you can decide you don't want to go to school

- give up all forms of hygiene

Your job is to take care of your body and your mind.

CONSENT is permission for a specific action. Today we will discuss aspects of consent as it relates to your boundaries, as well as the boundaries of others. Consent begins with respect. Consent is knowing that every person has the right to decide what happens to their body. Everyday you are setting your own boundaries and recognizing the boundaries of others.

This book will explain the importance of BOTH aspects of consent:

Setting Boundaries

Respecting the Boundaries of Others

WHAT IS CONSENT?

Section 1

My Body, My Boundaries

My Body, My Boundaries

Keeping your body healthy includes hygiene, eating right and getting exercise. It also includes setting healthy boundaries for yourself. It is your right to decide what you are and aren't comfortable with. It is also your right to voice those boundaries with others.

Read the statements below and circle True or False

You are allowed to set your own boundaries.   True   False

A doctor can touch your body without permission.   True   False

You can decide what happens to your body.   True   False

You can say "No" when it comes to your personal space.   True   False

You can do anything you want with your body.   True   False

I am my own person

What does MY BODY, My Rules mean?

Read each statement. Then write an example that relates to your life.

Making your own rules means you get to decide who touches your body.

_____
_____
_____

It includes knowing that you deserve privacy and to be treated with dignity and respect.

_____
_____
_____

Being in control of your own body means knowing that you can say "No" when you are uncomfortable.

_____
_____
_____

Setting your own boundaries for your body means you can decide how rough you want to play.

_____
_____
_____

Respecting your body means that you know your feelings are important.

_____
_____

Healthy Relationships

Friendships and relationships are both based on respecting each other and respecting each other's boundaries. Some boundaries involve personal space while others involve how people treat you. Voicing your opinions on what you think is and isn't appropriate is your right. Read the scenarios below and circle the statements that are in line with a healthy friendship/relationship.

The person you like tells you who you can and cannot talk to.

Complimenting the person you like.

Apologizing when you hurt someone's feelings.

The person you like ignores you in front of other people.

Someone who makes you feel good about yourself.

Someone who cares about your opinion and your feelings.

When he/she gets angry, he/she hurts you.

When someone is nice in private but not when others are around.

Someone who respects your boundaries.

When he/she doesn't take 'No' for an answer

Expectations

Every day we are exposed to ideas of what we *should* look like or how we *should* act. Commercials can make us think we are hungry. TV shows tell us what kind of relationship we *should* have. Some movies even convince us what we should be wearing. Don't think movies or TV change the way we act?

In 1934 Clark Gable appeared in a movie and after one scene, he tanked an entire industry.

Gable in *It Happened One Night*

After Mr. Gable took off his shirt in "It Happened One Night" and Claudette, like Euclid, looked on beauty bare, the undershirt demand dipped by percentages ranging up to an estimated 50.

Sales drop 50% according to this article found in the August 14, 1949 edition of the Pittsburgh Post Gazette:

How do you think media can affect how we think about our bodies and about sex?

_____

_____

Expectations

Read the statements below and discuss how each could negatively affect someone.

Boys need to feel strong. Girls will get more attention if they are in distress..

Boys who cry are considered weak.

Girls only need a makeover in order to impress the guy of their dreams.

Women just want to get married and men just want sex.

It's a good idea to change who you are for the one you love.

Everyone has sex on Prom night.

Kissing someone as a surprise is romantic.

Some TV and movies perpetuate narratives that lead young people to believe they should act a certain way about their bodies and relationships.

The truth is that **men are not animals** who have a primal urge for sex anymore than women do. Men have the ability to control their own actions just like women. And both men and women are allowed to say 'no' if they are uncomfortable.

Other than TV and movies, where else are we exposed to expectations?

_____

What are some other expectations you feel?

_____
_____
_____
_____

FINDING YOUR VOICE

Angelica and her best friend, Maria, were both asked to the Junior High dance by boys in their class. On the way to the dance, Angelica's date has his hand on her knee. As they get closer to the dance, his hand moves higher up her leg. Angelica doesn't want to ruin their evening but she isn't comfortable with him touching her in this way. As they arrive at the dance, Angelica's date whispers "just wait until we get inside." What can Angelica do?

- Angelica begins to question herself. Maybe she misheard him. Maybe his hand moving up her leg was not on purpose. Maybe she is misreading the situation. What can she do?

- On the way into the dance, Angelica pulls Maria into the bathroom and confides in her. Maria can tell that Angelica is uncomfortable. Maria suggests that she just try to avoid being alone with her date. Is this good advice?

- Angelica tries avoiding her date most of the night. Near the end of the dance, Angelica's date pulls her onto the dance floor for a slow dance. She doesn't want to be rude so she stays and dances with him. He tries putting his hand on her butt. Angelica tells him to stop. He tells Angelica that if he had known she would be a prude, he wouldn't have wasted his night by bringing her to the dance. Now Angelica feels obligated to spend the rest of the night with him. What can she do?

- As the dance ends, Maria's mother picks them up to drive the four of them home. Angelica's date offers to walk her home instead. What can she do?

FINDING YOUR VOICE

(Use this page to make notes on Angelica's scenario)

Boundaries *setting*

Speaking up can be difficult. Voicing your opinion when you are being disrespected is your right. Read the statements below and discuss how you would react.

- At a sleepover, your friend wants to stay up all night but you are very tired. What do you do?

- Your best friend dares you to use the hottest hot sauce on your lunch. You don't like spicy food but you don't want to be called a wimp. What do you do?

- You are the last person in your class to never have been kissed. The student you have a crush on says you should just kiss and get it over with. What do you do?

- All of the girls in your class have started wearing lipstick and you are being teased because you don't want to wear any. What do you do?

- Your friend always sits closer to you than you are comfortable with. What do you do?

> Do you think everyone has the same boundaries as you do?

> Do you have the same boundaries with all people?

REVIEW

1. It is my right to voice my opinions about what happens to my body.   True   False

2. Setting boundaries includes how I allow people to treat me.   True   False

3. Social narratives cannot affect how I view my sexuality or my body.   True   False

4. When I am uncomfortable, I should MAKE SURE before talking to a trusted adult.   True   False

5. Everyone has different boundaries for their bodies.   True   False

Section 2

Respecting Boundaries

SIGNALS
Recognizing and respecting the boundaries is not a guessing game.

When you were younger, playing with your friends was trial and error when it came to how rough someone wanted to play. Toddlers are not asking for consent before they tackle one another.

As you got older, reading social cues helped you know when you were playing too rough. Reading body language and knowing what you know about the person helped you along the way.

Now the stakes are higher as you navigate dating and sexuality. There is not room for trial and error when it comes to crossing the line with someone physically or sexually. "I thought he wanted me to" is not an excuse when it comes to sexual activity. Reading signals is **NOT A SUBSTITUTE** for having consent.

Consent is not about assuming you know what someone wants. Consent is not about what someone wanted yesterday. Consent is the permission you get for an action **EVERY SINGLE TIME.**

Consent is as easy as pie!

Easy As Pie

- You offer your friend some pie. He says "no thanks." Then you don't have pie.
- You offer your friend some pie. He says "Sure, I'd love some." You both have pie.

Both of these scenarios show **asking for consent** and respecting the answer. If consent was that easy, we wouldn't need a whole book on it. Read the following statements and decide what behaviors are exhibited in each.

Consent or No Consent   Respecting Boundaries   Assault   Abuse of Power

Voicing Boundaries   Pressuring   Disrespecting Boundaries

1. You offer your friend some pie. He says he's not sure. You slice two pieces of pie, knowing he might not want it. You again offer it to him and he decides he would like some pie. _____

2. Your friend offers you some pie. You say "no thanks". Then your friend pulls out a knife and orders you to eat the pie. _____

3. You offer your friend some pie. He says he had a big lunch and isn't hungry. You tell your friend that you spent all day making this pie and now he has ruined your evening by not eating any. _____

4. You offer your friend some pie. He says "yes." While you are getting the slices of pie, your friend falls asleep. You know he wanted the pie, so you decide to feed it to him while he is sleeping. _____

5. Your friend offers you some pie. You eat the pie and would like seconds. She says she's saving the rest for after dinner. But you are still hungry and so get yourself some more pie from the kitchen while your friend isn't looking.

_____
_____
_____
_____

6. Your friend offers you some pie. You don't really like pie and you don't want any but you think it would be rude to turn it down so you say "yes".

_____
_____
_____

7. You are at your friend's house and she doesn't offer you any pie. You think it's very rude to invite someone over and not have any desserts. You tell her you expected pie. You leave angry.

_____
_____
_____
_____

Critical Thinking

Why is it important to set your own boundaries and to voice those boundaries?

_____

What is the difference between wanting pie and not wanting pie but saying "ok I'll have some pie"?

_____

Trying to convince someone to give you a slice of pie is NOT the same as forcing them to give you pie or stealing pie while they aren't looking. But is it respectful of their boundaries?

_____
_____

If someone keeps asking for pie and you repeatedly say "no", what can you do? Is this the type of friend you want to have?

_____
_____

Boundaries *respecting*

Recognizing when you do and do NOT have consent is VITAL! Even if something is "Just a Joke", crossing the line without consent is a violation of boundaries. Read the statements below and discuss as a class.

- The boy you like has been paying more attention to you recently and you are sure he likes you. After school while he's waiting for the bus, you decide to just *Go For It* and kiss him.

- You are the captain of the football team. Your teammates are standing around while the trainer is taping your ankle. You think it would funny to pull down your shorts and moon the trainer. When the coach asks you about this behavior, you responded "it was just harmless fun."

- You have been dating someone for almost a year now. He/she has made it clear that he/she is not ready for any sexual activity except for kissing. You think you can get him/her in the mood to go further if you watch pornography together. So you send video clips to his/her phone.

- You are auditioning for the school play. Your scene involves flirting with your costar. You think the scene is more realistic if you kiss your costar to get genuine surprise in your audition.

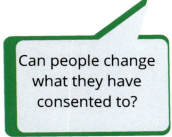

Can people change what they have consented to?

Should your friends be ok with something just because you are?

REVIEW

1. I must respect boundaries of everyone around me. True   False

2. When you are dating someone, that means they have already consented to things like kissing and hand holding. True   False

3. It can't be wrong if it was just "harmless fun". True   False

4. If you are not sure about what to do, you can talk to your trusted adult. True   False

5. The best way to know what someone is comfortable with is to just ask. True   False

6. Only men are capable of crossing the line and violating someone's boundaries. True   False

Section 3

Sexual Assault

What is Sexual Assault?

When you take "pie" out of the metaphor and add words like "kissing" or "touching" or "sex," these scenarios might seem more complicated. But the idea is the same. Consent is needed everytime. Boundaries need to be voiced and respected. Failure to respect those boundaries **IS A CRIME.**

Sexual Assault (n.)

Illegal sexual contact without consent that may involve: 1. physical force. 2. being inflicted upon a person who is incapable of giving consent (as because of age or physical or mental incapacity) or 3. the use of authority or trust to coerce a victim.

When is someone UNABLE to consent to sexual activity:

1.

2.

3.

4.

Which pie examples show the use of physical force?

Which pie examples show someone's inability to consent?

Now let's discuss the use of authority.

Abuse of Authority and Trust

If someone uses his/her power or authority to make a victim believe they have no other choice but to have sex, this is sexual assault. Abuses of power or trust can include misleading a victim under the guise of being an expert, threatening someone's job or safety, or simply taking advantage of someone significantly younger than they are. Any person in a position that is looked up to or respected can be in a position to abuse their authority. This does NOT mean that all people in power will abuse it. But being aware that it is possible, we can be more apt to listen with our gut when we are uncomfortable. Let's explore some examples:

- Christine is spending her summer interning in order to earn a letter of recommendation for her college applications. As the summer comes to an end, Christine's boss asks her out for dinner. Christine doesn't think that would be appropriate so she declines. Her boss says that if she doesn't have time for dinner, he doesn't think he will have time to write her a recommendation letter. What can Christine do?

- Gavin is getting fitted for a suit for his older brother's wedding. While measuring his inseam, the tailor gropes Gavin's penis over his pants. Gavin was very uncomfortable and asks the tailor not to touch him like that. The tailor tells Gavin that this is the way to get an accurate measurement. Gavin doesn't know what the normal procedure is for measuring inseams so he believes him and suffers through the uncomfortable experience. What can Gavin do?

- Elaina is a competitive diver in high school. She has had the same diving coach for more than 10 years. Her coach is one of her trusted adults. During a private practice, Elaina's coach tells her that diving without a bathing suit will help with her technique. Elaina has no reason to question her coach. What can Elaina do?

Between 2009-2013

63,000 US children are victims of sexual abuse **EACH YEAR**

*United States Department of Health and Human Services, Administration for Children and Families, Administration on Children, Youth and Families, Children's Bureau. Child Maltreatment Survey, 2012

What Do I Do Now?

If you have been sexually assaulted, your safety is the highest priority. Getting away from the perpetrator should be your first step. Find someone you can trust. Call a parent or trusted adult.

You may be told to preserve physical evidence, which includes not showering or changing clothes. If you have already showered, don't allow this to deter you from reporting the crime.

Reporting sexual assault is not easy. It's a decision that you may need help making. Once you are safe and have a trusted adult with you, you can explore your options and what steps to take.

Get to a Safe Place

Find someone you can trust.

Preserve evidence.

Report the crime.

Keep in mind that these are just guidelines. Sometimes victims don't realize they have been victimized until months or years later. Shock may have set in and a victim has already showered. Distance yourself from the perpetrator and find someone you can trust.

Safety is your first concern.

You Are Believed.

Out of every 1,000 sexual assaults, 310 are reported to the police. Why do you think some people choose not to report?

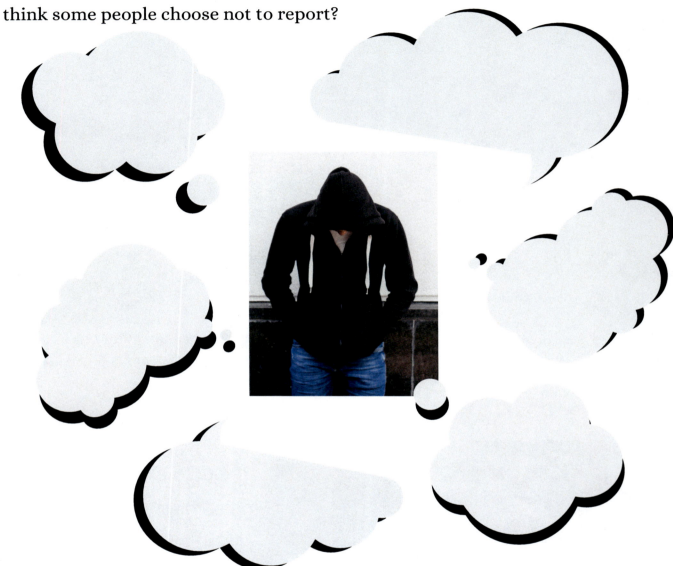

Reporting an assault can seem overwhelming. Victims may feel embarrassed or hesitant to share due to a number of reasons. You need to know that the crime was **NOT YOUR FAULT.**

You are believed. Find someone you trust. Tell someone. Because we believe you.

YOU ARE BELIEVED.

If you think you need help, YOU HAVE OPTIONS!

Find and adult you can trust. Talk to your Consent teacher right now. If you don't know who to turn to, here are some options for you.

National Sexual Assault Hotline   800.656.HOPE (4673)
Speak with a trained staff member from a local sexual assault service provider in your area.

Crisis Text Line is free, 24/7 support for those in crisis. Text **HOME to 741741** from anywhere in the US to text with a trained Crisis Counselor.

Childhelp National Child Abuse Hotline   800-4-A-CHILD (800-422-4453)
All calls are anonymous. The hotline counselors don't know who you are and you don't have to tell them.

Review

Let's discuss these Disney movies and decide which topics regarding CONSENT, ABUSE and BOUNDARIES are shown..

Disney's Frozen
"I could kiss you. I could. I mean, I'd like to. We me? I mean, may we? Wait, what?" -Kristoff
"We may." -Anna

Disney's Beauty and the Beast
"You'll join me for dinner. That's not a request." Belle refuses.
"You'll come out or I'll break down the door." -Beast

Disney's Tangled
"No. You were wrong about the world, and you were wrong about me, and I will never let you use my hair again!"
-Rapunzel to Mother Gothel

Disney's Snow White
The Prince kisses Snow White while she is sleeping.

Disney's Lion King
Simba asked his uncle, Scar, what he should do after his father died. Scar tells his only option is to run away.

This page is intended to help start the conversation of consent between their trusted adult and the children.

This page is meant to start a conversation between you and a trusted adult. Discuss what you learned in this booklet with an adult. Ask any questions and voice any concerns regarding boundaries or consent that you may have.

Discuss both aspects of consent:

Setting Boundaries for Yourself
Respecting the Boundaries of Others
Discuss a plan of action if you are in trouble.

Note to parent/adult:

This book is intended to teach students how to respect others and how to set their own boundaries. By talking to children about consent and sexual assault, we can empower them to know what is right and wrong more than any generation before. The most important three words you can say when someone comes to you with important information are "I BELIEVE YOU."

I, _____, agree to be open and as honest as possible when I feel
      (student)
that I am in need. I know that my body is my own. And I have people I can trust when I need help. I have the right to set my own boundaries and it is my duty to voice those boundaries. I will do my best to respect the boundaries of others. And I will talk to a trusted adult when I have questions.

I, _____, promise to listen with an open mind when you have
      (adult)
questions or concerns. You can talk to me even when you are scared. I am here to support you and to listen to you. Above all, I'm here to believe you, even when you think no one will.

As you go through the booklet in class, you may have questions that you only want to ask in private. Please use this page to write down questions or comments to be discussed later with your trusted adult or with your teacher at a later time.

(If you don't have questions, use this page to write about how COOL CONSENT is!)

Made in the USA
Coppell, TX
08 April 2022

76258917R00029